The Twelve
of Chri

Volume

Candlestick Press

Published by:
Candlestick Press,
21 Devonshire Avenue, Beeston,
Nottingham NG9 1BS, UK
www.candlestickpress.co.uk

Design, typesetting, print and production by DiVersity Creative
Marketing Solutions Ltd., www.diversity-nottm.co.uk

ISBN 978-1-907598-00-5

Acknowledgements:
Carol Ann Duffy and Candlestick Press would like to thank
Vivien Hamilton for her researches.

Thanks are due to Moniza Alvi ('Delhi Christmas' from *Split World:
Poems 1990-2005*, Bloodaxe Books, 2005), Connie Bensley ('Mr and
Mrs R and the Christmas Card List' from *Choosing to be a Swan*,
Bloodaxe Books, 1994), Gillian Clarke ('Shepherd' from *Making the
Beds for the Dead*, Carcanet Press, 2004),Wendy Cope ('The Christmas
Life' from *If I Don't Know*, Faber & Faber, 2001) the Estate of Elizabeth
Jennings ('Alone Over Christmas' from *New Collected Poems*, Carcanet
Press, 2002), Geoffrey Hill ('Picture of a Nativity' from *Collected
Poems*, Penguin Books, 1985. Copyright © Geoffrey Hill, 1985. First
published in *For The Unfallen*, copyright © Geoffrey Hill, 1959) and
Carol Ann Duffy for 'The Single Bed' printed here for the first time.
'A Christmas Childhood' by Patrick Kavanagh is reprinted from
Collected Poems ed. Antoinette Quinn (Allen Lane, 2004) by kind
permission of the Trustees of the Estate of the late Katherine B.
Kavanagh, through the Jonathan Williams Literary Agency.

The publisher offers special thanks to Carol Ann Duffy for her
generous help.

Where poets are no longer living, their dates are given.

Introduction

Here is the second of *The Twelve Poems of Christmas* series which I'll be selecting every year that I'm Poet Laureate for the scrumptious and innovative Candlestick Press. We enter this Christmas 2010 with, like Scrooge's encounter with The Ghost of Christmas Yet To Come, plenty to worry about – cuts and unemployment in our own country, our soldiers still fighting far from home, and so many of the year's traumas visibly unhealed, not least the people of Haiti still waiting for help to rebuild their lives and, more recently, the millions in Pakistan whose lives have been destroyed by the floods there. Candlestick Press will be making a donation to the British Red Cross out of the proceeds of this pamphlet which is, for me, a labour of love. Because, far from being irrelevant or superfluous, poetry is all the more vital and central at Christmas, as our joyful singing of our favourite carols – be we believers or not – noisily demonstrates.

Poetry – like Christmas – reminds us why we should never stop caring about each other and the world. It affirms things that matter and calls into question what needs to be scrutinised. Some of the poems chosen this year make us laugh, as Connie Bensley's wicked gem of a poem demonstrates. Others show the vulnerability of our world and the implications of our choices or offer new perspectives on our familiar rituals, as Moniza Alvi's poem does. There's so much pressure on people to come up with the perfect Christmas that these poems, I hope, will be time out for both giver and recipient and also assert how it's often the surprising, little things we encounter that matter more than all the hype and all the money, as Scrooge himself came to know.

Merry Christmas!

Carol Ann Duffy

Contents

The Christmas Life

'If you don't have a real tree, you don't bring the Christmas life
into the house.'

Josephine Mackinnon, aged 8

Bring in a tree, a young Norwegian spruce,
Bring hyacinths that rooted in the cold.
Bring winter jasmine as its buds unfold –
Bring the Christmas life into this house.

Bring red and green and gold, bring things that shine,
Bring candlesticks and music, food and wine.
Bring in your memories of Christmas past.
Bring in your tears for all that you have lost.

Bring in the shepherd boy, the ox and ass,
Bring in the stillness of an icy night,
Bring in a birth, of hope and love and light.
Bring the Christmas life into this house.

Wendy Cope

A Christmas Childhood

I

One side of the potato-pits was white with frost –
How wonderful that was, how wonderful!
And when we put our ears to the paling-post
The music that came out was magical.

The light between the ricks of hay and straw
Was a hole in Heaven's gable. An apple tree
With its December-glinting fruit we saw –
O you, Eve, were the world that tempted me

To eat the knowledge that grew in clay
And death the germ within it! Now and then
I can remember something of the gay
Garden that was childhood's. Again

The tracks of cattle to a drinking-place,
A green stone lying sideways in a ditch
Or any common sight the transfigured face
Of a beauty that the world did not touch.

II

My father played the melodeon
Outside at our gate;
There were stars in the morning east
And they danced to his music.

Across the wild bogs his melodeon called
To Lennons and Callans,
As I pulled on my trousers in a hurry
I knew some strange thing had happened.

Outside in the cow-house my mother
Made the music of milking;
The light of her stable-lamp was a star
And the frost of Bethlehem made it twinkle.

A water-hen screeched in the bog,
Mass-going feet
Crunched the wafer-ice on the pot-holes,
Somebody wistfully twisted the bellows wheel.

My child poet picked out the letters
On the grey stone,
In silver the wonder of a Christmas townland,
The winking glitter of a frosty dawn.

Cassiopeia was over
Cassidy's hanging hill,
I looked and three whin bushes rode across
The horizon – the Three Wise Kings.

An old man passing said:
'Can't he make it talk' –
The melodeon. I hid in the doorway
And tightened the belt of my box-pleated coat.

I nicked six nicks on the door-post
With my penknife's big blade –
There was a little one for cutting tobacco.
And I was six Christmases of age.

My father played the melodeon,
My mother milked the cows,
And I had a prayer like a white rose pinned
On the Virgin Mary's blouse.

Patrick Kavanagh (1904-1967)

Shepherd

Christmas, and over the snow
a jet chases the day,
cresting the sill of the land
to take the Atlantic.

In the fields
a man and his dog
check the sheep dawn and dusk
as they've always done.

What's it to him,
the flight of kings,
but to remind him
that the world turns,

that going home is a prayer,
that even war draws breath.

Gillian Clarke

Mr and Mrs R and the Christmas Card List

Shall I cross them off?
It's twenty years since we last met.

Of course Mr R and I once thought
we were made for each other –

Ah, that heart-stopping moment
by the kitchen sink, when he took off

his spectacles and fiercely kissed me.
But all that lasted less than a week

And what I recall more vividly
Is Mrs R's good advice:

Always plunge your lemons in hot water
before you squeeze them.

One more year perhaps.

Connie Bensley

Delhi Christmas

In hotel lobbies skinny Christmas trees
rest on beds of egg-white satin

hold blunt finger-strips of cotton wool.
Santa gestures like a tour leader

next to log cabin, jewelled caravan.
Piano and cello send incessant *Jingle Bells*

into the costly international atmosphere.
And *The Times of India* hosts recipes

for 'ginger hut' and marzipan.
Inhabitants of silent corridors – the workers

murmur Merry Christmas, nod and smile.
Fierce air-conditioning creates a winter chill.

Sunbathers, indolent, line the swimming pool,
while England floats contained, so far away

like a glass-domed scene with shaken snow.
Cliff-like in the cool night air

Eastern hotels tap lightly into Christmas.
English couples talk of cats in Abingdon.

Moniza Alvi

Alone Over Christmas

A serious night of calm it is. The moon
More than half. How warm it is for Winter.
Christmas will be on us very soon.
It is the time of Advent Calendars
    And I sit down alone

Happy and full of friendship but I think
Of a young man who at the weekend stood
Calling 'Everyone's walking past.' Some brink
Of lonely terror was near him. It's no good
    Pretending every link

Between each human being and another
At Christmas suddenly grows firm and solid.
This lonely man is everybody's brother
And we *do* walk past in selfish mood
    Not bothering to bother.

Elizabeth Jennings (1926-2001)

Karma

Christmas was in the air and all was well
With him, but for a few confusing flaws
In divers of God's images. Because
A friend of his would neither buy nor sell,
Was he to answer for the axe that fell?
He pondered; and the reason for it was,
Partly, a slowly freezing Santa Claus
Upon the corner, with his beard and bell.

Acknowledging an improvident surprise,
He magnified a fancy that he wished
The friend whom he had wrecked were here again.
Not sure of that, he found a compromise;
And from the fullness of his heart he fished
A dime for Jesus who had died for men.

Edwin Arlington Robinson (1869-1935)

The Oxen

Christmas Eve, and twelve of the clock,
  'Now they are all on their knees,'
An elder said as we sat in a flock
  By the embers in hearthside ease.

We pictured the meek mild creatures where
  They dwelt in their strawy pen,
Nor did it occur to one of us there
  To doubt they were kneeling then.

So fair a fancy few would weave
  In these years! Yet, I feel,
If someone said on Christmas Eve
  'Come; see the oxen kneel

In the lonely barton by yonder coomb
  Our childhood used to know,'
I should go with him in the gloom,
  Hoping it might be so.

Thomas Hardy (1840-1928)

Winter

Clouded with snow
The cold winds blow,
And shrill on leafless bough
The robin with its burning breast
Alone sings now.

The rayless sun,
Day's journey done,
Sheds its last ebbing light
On fields in leagues of beauty spread
Unearthly white.

Thick draws the dark,
And spark by spark,
The frost-fires kindle, and soon
Over that sea of frozen foam
Floats the white moon.

Walter de la Mare (1873-1956)

The Starlight Night

Look at the stars! look, look up at the skies!
  O look at all the fire-folk sitting in the air!
  The bright boroughs, the circle-citadels there!
Down in dim woods the diamond delves! the elves'-eyes!

The grey lawns cold where gold, where quickgold lies!
  Wind-beat whitebeam! airy abeles set on a flare!
  Flake-doves sent floating forth at a farmyard scare! –
Ah well! It is all a purchase, all is a prize.

Buy then! bid then! – What? – Prayer, patience, alms, vows.
Look, look: a May-mess, like on orchard boughs!
  Look! March-bloom, like on mealed-with-yellow sallows!
These are indeed the barn; withindoors house
The shocks. This piece-bright paling shuts the spouse
  Christ home, Christ and his mother and all his hallows.

Gerard Manley Hopkins (1844-1889)

Picture Of A Nativity

Sea-preserved, heaped with sea-spoils,
Ribs, keels, coral sores,
Detached faces, ephemeral oils,
Discharged on the world's outer shores,

A dumb child-king
Arrives at his right place; rests,
Undisturbed, among slack serpents; beasts
With claws flesh-buttered. In the gathering

Of bestial and common hardship
Artistic men appear to worship
And fall down; to recognize
Familiar tokens; believe their own eyes.

Above the marvel, each rigid head,
Angels, their unnatural wings displayed,
Freeze into an attitude
Recalling the dead.

Geoffrey Hill

The Single Bed

was first a wooden boat;
stars translated for me
as I drifted away –
our cargoed winter house
dark and at anchor –

and then a Russian Doll
where I stilled in my selves,
six secrets or presents
under a thrilled tree.

I saw a coffin once,
shouldered through snow, shrouded,
a last bed with its sheet.
Now, delirious bells
shaking the small spare room
on Christmas morning.

Carol Ann Duffy

This is the second volume in a series of ten poetry pamphlets published in collaboration with Carol Ann Duffy and celebrating Christmas for each year of her laureateship.

A few copies of the first volume of *The Twelve Poems of Christmas* are still available from Candlestick Press.